A Mouthful of Miracles

A Mouthful of Miracles

The Power of Speaking God's Word

Philip Hutchings

Scriptures marked KJV are taken from the KING JAMES VERSION (KJV): KING JAMES VERSION, public domain.

Scriptures marked NLT are taken from the HOLY BIBLE, NEW LIVING TRANSLATION (NLT): Scriptures taken from the HOLY BIBLE, NEW LIVING TRANSLATION, Copyright© 1996, 2004, 2007 by Tyndale House Foundation. Used by permission of Tyndale House Publishers, Inc., Carol Stream, Illinois 60188. All rights reserved. Used by permission.

Scripture quotations marked AMPC are taken from the Amplified® Bible, Copyright © 1954, 1958, 1962, 1964, 1965, 1987 by The Lockman Foundation. Used by permission. lockman.org.

Book design by eBook Prep
www.ebookprep.com

April 2023
ISBN: 978-1-64457-595-6

Rise UP Publications
644 Shrewsbury Commons Ave
Ste 249
Shrewsbury PA 17361
United States of America

www.riseUPpublications.com
Phone: 866-846-5123

Contents

Acknowledgments

I would be careless if I failed to acknowledge Charles Capps and the impact his teaching has made on my life and ministry. Any copying of his phrasing or thoughts will be unavoidable.

Why You Need this Book

Because you use words every day, you have no choice but to follow what you say.

Believe it or not, both Scripture and science show that your life will follow your mouth. YOU HAVE NO CHOICE BUT TO FOLLOW YOUR WORDS. But you do have a choice of what you say.

With that in mind, this book is an interruption. I want you to stop for a moment and see why words are powerful. Then I want to help you make favorable adjustments. If you catch hold of this revelation and implement the tools I'm throwing at you, you will speedily see results.

When you take control of your words, you take back your life. If your words are in line with the Word of God, Satan can't touch you.

So, this book is important!

I pray this revelation will do for you what it has done for me.

Chapter One

Religious People Hate This

L et's cut to the chase.

Religious people dislike this. When I speak of "religious people," I mean people who embrace religious ceremonies more than they revere Christ.

Christianity isn't a religion. Religion is man's attempt to get to God. But Christianity is a relationship where God came to us. Religious people don't become empty and "religious" overnight. It starts slowly by moving from the pure Word of God to tradition. And Jesus warns us about it in Mark chapter 7. It can cause an individual to "cancel and nullify the power and effect of the Word of God" on their life. So now, any message that truly carries power becomes an indictment of their powerless living.

Sadly, I find that some "religious" circles target anything which carries power, or what they misunderstand, with mockery and labeling.

For example, when I preach from the Bible concerning the power of words, it's then labeled "the name it and claim it" preaching and teaching. People will say how they dislike the "positive confession" preaching. I guess ignorance would prefer the "negative confession" preaching.

In reality, what I'm sharing is not about positive confession as it is about "Bible confession"...confessing specifically God's Word. It's not necessarily about sounding like a Hallmark card every time you speak, but it is about sounding like Jesus when you speak.

It's about speaking, yes. But specifically speaking God's word!

How many reading this right now agree that God's Word is powerful?

Most of you, I'm sure.

Well, how powerful would it be if you gave voice to the Word of God? THINK ABOUT IT. Really think about that.

Also, sometimes people only connect "confession" to when you make a mistake and must then confess your sin before the Lord. Well, that's only one side of that confession coin. There's also the power of confessing the Word of God.

Let's dig in!

Chapter Two

The Construction Center of Your Life

You must settle the fact that words frame and build.

Your vocabulary is like a hardware store, carrying everything you need to build and construct. Your mouth is the production center of your life and family.

Proverbs 18:20 tells us we eat the "fruit" of our mouths. Think about that. "The fruit of his mouth" references production and creation.

Your mouth is framing something.

Your mouth is producing something.

Every word you speak is a seed. When you speak, you're planting.

So, the sobering question is: what are you planting and sowing with your words?

What are you producing with what you say? Words have creative power. They will produce something.

We see that in Genesis at the start of everything. The first picture we see of our heavenly father is Him starting everything with words!

"light be."

"and it was so."

The Bible opens by presenting an almighty god who creates the universe by his "spoken word."

Psalm 33 tells us clearly that by the spoken Word, it was created. By the *"spoken"* Word. Think about that. It doesn't say by the "unspoken" Word of God.

Genesis 1:3 - GOD *SAID*...AND *IT WAS* SO.

Genesis 1:6 - GOD SAID...AND IT WAS SO.

Genesis 1:9 - GOD SAID...AND IT WAS SO.

Genesis 1:11 - GOD SAID...AND IT WAS SO.

Genesis 1:14 - GOD SAID...AND IT WAS SO.

Genesis 1:20 - GOD SAID...AND IT WAS SO.

Genesis 1:24 - GOD SAID...AND IT WAS SO.

So, what's the point?

When you open your mouth and speak God's Word over your country and over your home, God's miracle-working power will explode in your life, bringing a new beginning, much like we see in creation with our Heavenly Father.

Hallelujah!

Just think about this for a minute. God said, *"light be"* and 24 hours later, there were billions of miles of the universe.

Never forget that we live in a *word-created* and *word-dominated* world. God spoke it, and it was so. So it is with you. The Bible says, "let the redeemed say so" (Psalm 107:2 TRAN). Every time you say so, it's so.

You may ask: Are you suggesting talking like it is so? ...even when it's not so?

YES...Because God did!

And Ephesians 5:1 tells us to imitate our Father in all we do.

God spoke what wasn't there. He spoke what He wanted to see, not to describe what He was currently seeing. Romans 4:17 reminds us He is a God who *calls those things that be not, as though they are.*

As you study the Bible, you will notice God does nothing until He says it. That's the way He works. God has done nothing in the earth without first speaking it.

Even now, God will do nothing in the earth unless it is spoken, prophesied, or called for by the prayer of faith.

Chapter Three

Did Jesus Lie About Lazarus?

Think about the life of Jesus. When you study His life, you find several important facts that caused Him to overcome.

His conversation always consisted of what the Father said. He always spoke the end results, not the problem.

He never confessed present circumstances. He spoke the desired results. And Jesus was misunderstood because of His confession. And you may be misunderstood as you confess the results you desire to see. Just don't waste your time trying to explain yourself to those who are determined to misunderstand you.

Remember Lazarus?

> ...therefore, his sisters sent unto him, saying, lord, behold, he whom thou lovest is sick. When Jesus heard that, he said, "this sickness is not unto death, but for the glory of god, that the son of god might be glorified thereby.
>
> — John 11:3-4 (KJV)

Jesus said, *"this sickness is not unto death."*

What are you going to do with that statement?

Reading further, you find out that Lazarus died. And Jesus said that this sickness was not unto death, but for the glory of God, that the son of God might be glorified.

Some say, "Jesus said that Lazarus was sick and died so that God would be glorified." But it wasn't God's will for Lazarus to be sick. Neither was it God's will for Lazarus to die.

So, there is a difference between a lie and calling things that are not. What was Jesus saying? Was He telling a lie? Of course not! A lie is a sin, and the Bible says there was no sin in him (1 John 3:5).

So, what was Jesus doing?

Jesus was calling the end results of the matter.

He said that the result would not be death, but the result of this whole matter would bring glory to God. God's glory came when Lazarus was raised from the dead, not when he was sick or died.

Neither sickness nor death ever glorifies God. *The resurrection glorified God.* God raised him from the dead. Hallelujah!

If it was God's will for Lazarus to die, then Jesus destroyed the work of His father when He raised him from the dead. However, Jesus came *"that he might destroy the works of the devil"* (1 John 3:8 (KJV).

So, Jesus destroyed the works of the Devil when He raised Lazarus from the dead. Bam!

If you follow Jesus in this account of Lazarus, you'll see something as he starts toward Bethany.

> These things said he: and after that he saith unto them, 'Our
> friend Lazarus sleepeth; but I go, that I may awake him out
> of sleep.' Then said his disciples, 'Lord, if he sleeps, he shall
> do well.' How be it Jesus spake of his death: but they
> thought that he had spoken of taking of rest in sleep.
>
> — John 11:11-13 (KJV)

Jesus realized they had misunderstood Him when the disciples said, "If Lazarus is asleep, he is doing well."

So, Jesus was calling the thing that was not. Lazarus wasn't asleep; he was dead, and Jesus knew he was dead.

On the way to Bethany, Jesus said, *"Lazarus is sleeping."* What was He doing?

He was guarding His conversation so he wouldn't undo what he had already declared in the beginning (*"the end results will not be death"*).

But his disciples misunderstood him. So, Jesus explained what was, but called what was not. And Jesus stopped and gave His followers an explanation *"Lazarus is dead"* (v.14).

That's the way the King James Version states it. But if you read the Interlinear Greek English New Testament or the Orthodox Jewish Bible, the word translated as "dead" in the King James Version is translated as "died."

There is a difference between someone who died and someone who is dead. If you don't understand that, look at Jesus. He *died*, but he is not *dead*.

Jesus called the thing that was not manifest. Lazarus was not asleep, He was dead, but Jesus called him *"asleep."*

Amazingly, Jesus would not admit death.

That didn't mean he denied it. He simply wouldn't establish anything other than what he declared when he heard the bad news.

So back to the account…

> Then they took away the stone from the place where the dead
> was laid. And Jesus lifted up his eyes, and said, father, I
> thank thee that thou hast heard me.
>
> — John 11:41 (KJV)

Notice Jesus hasn't said anything yet, but He is thanking God that He has heard Him. Jesus is referring to what He had previously spoken.

Basically, He was saying, *"Father, I thank you that You heard what I decreed by faith. And the end results will not end in death but bring glory to You."* We must learn and do this principle.

Jesus established end results. At the tomb of Lazarus, Jesus said to the Father, *"I thank you that you have heard me."* He has established something.

> …and I knew that you hear me always: but because of the
> people which stand by I said it, that they may believe that
> you have sent me
>
> — John 11:42 (KJV)

He said, "I knew you would hear me. That's the reason I said it. I wanted to establish this on Earth."

When you speak, you establish!

Chapter Four

Binding and Loosing

We know from Psalm 119:89 that God's Word is already established in Heaven, but on Earth is where it needs to be established now. That's where your mouth and your words come in.

Look at what Jesus said to Peter:

> And I will give unto thee the keys of the kingdom of heaven: and whatsoever thou shalt bind on earth shall be bound in heaven: and whatsoever thou shalt loose on earth shall be loosed in heaven.
>
> — Matthew 16:19 (KJV)

Jesus said the power of binding and loosing is on Earth. This is amazing.

You have authority to bind on Earth those things which have been bound out of Heaven. You can loose things on Earth, and God will loose the same in Heaven. But you must first take action on Earth.

Jesus loosed Lazarus from death.

> And when he thus had spoken, he cried with a loud voice,
> Lazarus, come forth.

> — John 11:43 (KJV)

Jesus spoke to things and they obeyed.

In Jesus' ministry, He talked to a tree. He talked to the wind. He talked to the sea…and they all obeyed Him. In every instance, He was *calling for things that were not manifest.*

You may feel like an idiot about what you are saying because the situation in the natural world looks contrary to what you're saying.

But when you call the promise of God into manifestation in your life, all the embarrassment will leave when you see God's Word made manifest in your life.

Chapter Five

Did Jesus Lie About Jairus' Daughter?

R ead the following passage and see if you notice something similar to what happened with Lazarus.

On the other side of the lake the crowds welcomed Jesus, because they had been waiting for him. Then a man named Jairus, a leader of the local synagogue, came and fell at Jesus' feet, pleading with him to come home with him. His only daughter, who was about twelve years old, was dying.

As Jesus went with him, he was surrounded by the crowds.

While he was still speaking to her, a messenger arrived from the home of Jairus, the leader of the synagogue. He told him, "Your daughter is dead. There's no use troubling the Teacher now."

But when Jesus heard what had happened, he said to Jairus, "Don't be afraid. Just have faith, and she will be healed."

When they arrived at the house, Jesus wouldn't let anyone go in with him except Peter, John, James, and the little girl's father and mother. The house was filled with people weeping and wailing, but he said, "Stop the weeping! She isn't dead; she's only asleep."

But the crowd laughed at him because they all knew she had died. Then Jesus took her by the hand and said in a loud voice, "My child, get up!" And at that moment her life returned, and she immediately stood up! Then Jesus told them to give her something to eat. Her parents were overwhelmed, but Jesus insisted that they not tell anyone what had happened.

— Luke 8:40-42, 49-56 (NLT)

Notice where Jesus said, *"She isn't dead, she is only sleeping."* There it is again. Jesus wasn't telling a lie, but rather speaking of the end result. It's a pattern throughout the Bible. You can't escape it.

So now, it's your turn. What do I mean?

God is backing your faith just as surely as He backed Jesus' faith. So, speak to your situation with authority. Speak confidently and speak the end result.

Think of speaking your words like pushing a start button. A start button sets in motion the process by which we receive the desired result.

The same is true in the spiritual realm when we speak words. We have a host of promises from God's Word that we can expect to see come to pass in our lives. But first, we must set our faith into motion by speaking and calling things the way we want them to be, not how they are.

It's time to stop telling it like it is and start telling it like the Word of God says it should be. When you continually speak the Word of God in the face of adversity, you will change your circumstances.

Refuse to let the Devil or the world influence your words. Stand firm in your decision to only speak what you want to see come to pass in your life. Speak God's Word and see Biblical results.

Chapter Six

How Many Words Do You Speak Each Day?

S ome sources claim an average guy speaks between 2000-3000 words per day and an average lady speaks between 10,000-20,000 words per day. So, let's say an average of 5000 words per day. That's much seed being sown.

The questions we need to answer are: How many of those words carry the life of God? Faith? Blessing? How many of those words carry defeat? Curse? Death?

When something big and problematic gets in our way, it's easy to use words to describe the situation, but it's time to use our words not to describe the mountain that's in our way but to *speak* to it.

Is there a mountain in your way?

In Mark 11:23 it says, *"if anyone SAYS to this mountain GO!"*

It doesn't say if anyone TALKS ABOUT this mountain. Settle the fact that words can put you over or put you under. Some people don't want to believe this is true because then they become responsible for what is going on in their own lives.

Many people want to blame the Devil or God's will for their problems, but the Bible teaches God has delegated authority here on Earth...TO YOU.

Your words have the authority to create every time you speak. If you only speak Biblical results in prayer and negative and doubtful results the rest of the time, your negative and doubtful words will produce. So, speak Biblical results in prayer and outside of prayer. Speak the desired result all the time.

Charles Capps once said that the Lord told him this: "I have told my people that they can have what they say, and they are saying what they have."

Wow! Think about that. Saying "what you have" has no power to change things.

Chapter Seven

David Used His Words Before He Used His Sling

R ead the following passage and really meditate on it…

The Philistines now mustered their army for battle and camped
between Socoh in Judah and Azekah at Ephes-dammim. Saul
countered by gathering his Israelite troops near the valley of
Elah. So the Philistines and Israelites faced each other on
opposite hills, with the valley between them.

Then Goliath, a Philistine champion from Gath, came out of the
Philistine ranks to face the forces of Israel. He was over nine
feet tall! He wore a bronze helmet, and his bronze coat of
mail weighed 125 pounds. He also wore bronze leg armor,
and he carried a bronze javelin on his shoulder. The shaft of
his spear was as heavy and thick as a weaver's beam, tipped
with an iron spearhead that weighed 15 pounds. His armor
bearer walked ahead of him carrying a shield.

Goliath stood and shouted a taunt across to the Israelites. "Why
are you all coming out to fight?" he called. "I am the Philistine champion, but you are only the servants of Saul. Choose
one man to come down here and fight me! If he kills me,

then we will be your slaves. But if I kill him, you will be our slaves! I defy the armies of Israel today! Send me a man who will fight me!" When Saul and the Israelites heard this, they were terrified and deeply shaken.

Jesse Sends David to Saul's Camp

Now David was the son of a man named Jesse, an Ephrathite from Bethlehem in the land of Judah. Jesse was an old man at that time, and he had eight sons. Jesse's three oldest sons —Eliab, Abinadab, and Shimea—had already joined Saul's army to fight the Philistines. David was the youngest son. David's three oldest brothers stayed with Saul's army, but David went back and forth so he could help his father with the sheep in Bethlehem.

For forty days, every morning and evening, the Philistine champion strutted in front of the Israelite army.

One day Jesse said to David, "Take this basket of roasted grain and these ten loaves of bread, and carry them quickly to your brothers. And give these ten cuts of cheese to their captain. See how your brothers are getting along, and bring back a report on how they are doing." David's brothers were with Saul and the Israelite army at the valley of Elah, fighting against the Philistines.

So David left the sheep with another shepherd and set out early the next morning with the gifts, as Jesse had directed him. He arrived at the camp just as the Israelite army was leaving for the battlefield with shouts and battle cries. Soon the Israelite and Philistine forces stood facing each other, army against army. David left his things with the keeper of supplies and hurried out to the ranks to greet his brothers. As he was talking with them, Goliath, the Philistine champion from Gath, came out from the Philistine ranks. Then David heard him shout his usual taunt to the army of Israel.

As soon as the Israelite army saw him, they began to run away in fright. "Have you seen the giant?" the men asked. "He comes out each day to defy Israel. The king has offered a huge reward to anyone who kills him. He will give that man one of his daughters for a wife, and the man's entire family will be exempted from paying taxes!"

David asked the soldiers standing nearby, "What will a man get for killing this Philistine and ending his defiance of Israel? Who is this pagan Philistine anyway, that he is allowed to defy the armies of the living God?"

And these men gave David the same reply. They said, "Yes, that is the reward for killing him."

But when David's oldest brother, Eliab, heard David talking to the men, he was angry. "What are you doing around here anyway?" he demanded. "What about those few sheep you're supposed to be taking care of? I know about your pride and deceit. You just want to see the battle!"

"What have I done now?" David replied. "I was only asking a question!" He walked over to some others and asked them the same thing and received the same answer. Then David's question was reported to King Saul, and the king sent for him.

David Kills Goliath

"Don't worry about this Philistine," David told Saul. "I'll go fight him!"

"Don't be ridiculous!" Saul replied. "There's no way you can fight this Philistine and possibly win! You're only a boy, and he's been a man of war since his youth."

But David persisted. "I have been taking care of my father's sheep and goats," he said. "When a lion or a bear comes to steal a lamb from the flock, I go after it with a club and rescue the lamb from its mouth. If the animal turns on me, I catch it by the jaw and club it to death. I have done this to both lions and bears, and I'll do it to this pagan Philistine, too, for he has defied the armies of the living God! The Lord who rescued me from the claws of the lion and the bear will rescue me from this Philistine!"

Saul finally consented. "All right, go ahead," he said. "And may the Lord be with you!"

Then Saul gave David his own armor—a bronze helmet and a coat of mail. David put it on, strapped the sword over it, and took a step or two to see what it was like, for he had never worn such things before.

"I can't go in these," he protested to Saul. "I'm not used to them." So David took them off again. He picked up five smooth stones from a stream and put them into his shepherd's bag. Then, armed only with his shepherd's staff and sling, he started across the valley to fight the Philistine.

Goliath walked out toward David with his shield bearer ahead of him, sneering in contempt at this ruddy-faced boy. "Am I a dog," he roared at David, "that you come at me with a stick?" And he cursed David by the names of his gods. "Come over here, and I'll give your flesh to the birds and wild animals!" Goliath yelled.

David replied to the Philistine, "You come to me with sword, spear, and javelin, but I come to you in the name of the Lord of Heaven's Armies—the God of the armies of Israel, whom you have defied. Today the Lord will conquer you, and I will kill you and cut off your head. And then I will give the dead bodies of your men to the birds and wild animals, and the whole world will know that there is a God in Israel! And everyone assembled here will know that the Lord rescues his people, but not with sword and spear. This is the Lord's battle, and he will give you to us!"

As Goliath moved closer to attack, David quickly ran out to meet him. Reaching into his shepherd's bag and taking out a stone, he hurled it with his sling and hit the Philistine in the forehead. The stone sank in, and Goliath stumbled and fell face down on the ground.

So David triumphed over the Philistine with only a sling and a stone, for he had no sword. Then David ran over and pulled Goliath's sword from its sheath. David used it to kill him and cut off his head.

— 1 Samuel 17:1-51 (NLT)

Before David threw the stone, he threw his words. He went even further with it and went into testimony time (vs.34-37). He started declaring how God delivered him before and that God would do it again. David was unique in his time, and because of it, he spoke differently and saw different results. You can do the same.

David had a different mouth from the majority. Notice that much of Israel's army was speaking about the giant rather than speaking to the giant. They were listing the statistics of the problem in front of them while David was listing off the statistics of his God.

Your feet will follow your mouth. Israel's mouth sent them on the run *from* Goliath, while David's mouth sent him on the run *to* Goliath and to victory.

Your mouth will either set you back or set you ahead.

Another thing to notice is that David never called Goliath a giant. He brought up the covenant and called him out. He said, "you uncircumcised Philistine." David was bringing up the covenant. David was speaking covenant. This is key. And it's key for you.

David not only established victory with his mouth. He also established the *when* with his mouth. He said *today,* Goliath was going down.

So, what's the point? Sometimes we hold the expiration date of our situation. As long as we keep calling things like they are, those things will never change!

Why do you think God tells us in His Word, "Let the weak *say* I am strong" (Joel 3:10 KJV)? God wants you to establish the desired result.

Chapter Eight

The Great Confession

Christianity is called The Great Confession.

Sadly, many Christians live defeated lives because they believe and confess the wrong things.

Proverbs 13:3 tells us that when you guard your lips, you actually guard your life.

Proverbs 6:1-2 reminds us that "your words snare you."

This is not a theory. This is a fact. This is a spiritual law. And much like the laws we see in the natural world like the Law of Gravity, there are spiritual laws. When you speak, you set spiritual laws in motion.

This isn't a call for positive confession. This is a call for biblical confession. It's time to let your words match God's Word, and make this spiritual law work for you.

Chapter Nine

The Woman from Shunam

This is another incredible example of the producing power of words.

And it fell on a day, that Elisha passed to Shunem, where was a great woman; and she constrained him to eat bread. And so it was, that as oft as he passed by, he turned in thither to eat bread.

And she said unto her husband, Behold now, I perceive that this is an holy man of God, which passeth by us continually.

Let us make a little chamber, I pray thee, on the wall; and let us set for him there a bed, and a table, and a stool, and a candlestick: and it shall be, when he cometh to us, that he shall turn in thither.

And it fell on a day, that he came thither, and he turned into the chamber, and lay there.

And he said to Gehazi his servant, Call this Shunammite. And when he had called her, she stood before him.

And he said unto him, Say now unto her, Behold, thou hast been careful for us with all this care; what is to be done for

thee? wouldest thou be spoken for to the king, or to the
captain of the host? And she answered, I dwell among mine
own people.

And he said, What then is to be done for her? And Gehazi
answered, Verily she hath no child, and her husband is old.

And he said, Call her. And when he had called her, she stood in
the door.

And he said, About this season, according to the time of life,
thou shalt embrace a son. And she said, Nay, my lord, thou
man of God, do not lie unto thine handmaid.

And the woman conceived, and bare a son at that season that
Elisha had said unto her, according to the time of life.

And when the child was grown, it fell on a day, that he went out
to his father to the reapers.

And he said unto his father, My head, my head. And he said to a
lad, Carry him to his mother.

And when he had taken him, and brought him to his mother, he
sat on her knees till noon, and then died.

And she went up, and laid him on the bed of the man of God,
and shut the door upon him, and went out.

And she called unto her husband, and said, Send me, I pray
thee, one of the young men, and one of the asses, that I may
run to the man of God, and come again.

And he said, Wherefore wilt thou go to him to day? it is
neither new moon, nor sabbath. And she said, It shall be
well.

Then she saddled an ass, and said to her servant, Drive, and go
forward; slack not thy riding for me, except I bid thee.

So she went and came unto the man of God to mount Carmel.
And it came to pass, when the man of God saw her afar off,
that he said to Gehazi his servant, Behold, yonder is that
Shunammite:

Run now, I pray thee, to meet her, and say unto her, Is it well with thee? is it well with thy husband? is it well with the child? And she answered, It is well:

And when she came to the man of God to the hill, she caught him by the feet: but Gehazi came near to thrust her away. And the man of God said, Let her alone; for her soul is vexed within her: and the Lord hath hid it from me, and hath not told me.

Then she said, Did I desire a son of my lord? did I not say, Do not deceive me?

Then he said to Gehazi, Gird up thy loins, and take my staff in thine hand, and go thy way: if thou meet any man, salute him not; and if any salute thee, answer him not again: and lay my staff upon the face of the child.

And the mother of the child said, As the Lord liveth, and as thy soul liveth, I will not leave thee. And he arose, and followed her.

And Gehazi passed on before them, and laid the staff upon the face of the child; but there was neither voice, nor hearing. Wherefore he went again to meet him, and told him, saying, The child is not awaked.

And when Elisha was come into the house, behold, the child was dead, and laid upon his bed.

He went in therefore, and shut the door upon them twain, and prayed unto the Lord.

And he went up, and lay upon the child, and put his mouth upon his mouth, and his eyes upon his eyes, and his hands upon his hands: and stretched himself upon the child; and the flesh of the child waxed warm.

Then he returned, and walked in the house to and fro; and went up, and stretched himself upon him: and the child sneezed seven times, and the child opened his eyes.

— 2 Kings 4:8-35 (KJV)

Philip Hutchings

ALL IS WELL.

ALL IS WELL.

ALL IS WELL.

Did she deny the situation? No. Faith doesn't deny the situation but denies the permission of that situation to have the final say. Like with Jesus, she wasn't lying. She was speaking about the end result.

Right now, declare "ALL IS WELL" over your life.

You must speak deliverance before you see deliverance. Your words don't just create, your words also grant permission. So, what are your words permitting into your life?

> Those who live in the shelter of the Most High
> will find rest in the shadow of the Almighty.
> This I declare about the Lord:
> He alone is my refuge, my place of safety;
>   he is my God, and I trust him.
> For he will rescue you from every trap
>   and protect you from deadly disease.
> He will cover you with his feathers.
>   He will shelter you with his wings.
>   His faithful promises are your armor and protection.
> Do not be afraid of the terrors of the night,
>   nor the arrow that flies in the day.
> Do not dread the disease that stalks in darkness,
>   nor the disaster that strikes at midday.
> Though a thousand fall at your side,
>   though ten thousand are dying around you,
>   these evils will not touch you.
> Just open your eyes,
>   and see how the wicked are punished.

If you make the Lord your refuge,
   if you make the Most High your shelter, no evil will conquer
     you;
   no plague will come near your home.
For he will order his angels
   to protect you wherever you go.
They will hold you up with their hands
   so you won't even hurt your foot on a stone.
You will trample upon lions and cobras;
   you will crush fierce lions and serpents under your feet!
The Lord says, "I will rescue those who love me.
   I will protect those who trust in my name.
When they call on me, I will answer;
   I will be with them in trouble.
   I will rescue and honor them.
I will reward them with a long life
   and give them my salvation."

— Psalm 91 (NLT)

Notice where it says: "I will DECLARE of the Lord."

Declare what? "That He is my refuge and my fortress." That, my friend, is a statement of faith!

Note where it says, "For He will save me." After you "say" deliverance, you will "see" deliverance. Words are like a start button. Like the start buttons on appliances, or cars, words are the same thing...they ignite something.

Chapter Ten

Is Satan Stealing from you?

Did you know words are also Satan's way of stealing from you?

Only it must be in faith that he asks with no wavering (no hesitating, no doubting). For the one who wavers (hesitates, doubts) is like the billowing surge out at sea that is blown hither and thither and tossed by the wind.

For truly, let not such a person imagine that he will receive anything [he asks for] from the Lord,

[For being as he is] a man of two minds (hesitating, dubious, irresolute), [he is] unstable and unreliable and uncertain about everything [he thinks, feels, decides].

— James 1:6-8 (AMPC)

James reminds us that there are only 2 options: WAVERING or RECEIVING

Satan knows this. So, Satan will pressure you to speak in agreement with him. He can't do anything without your cooperation. So, you need to resist him!

James 4:7 tells us to resist the Devil, and he will flee. But have you built up resistance? God's Word is the resistance.

Make everything you say agree with what God says. Be consistent in speaking faithful words. Husbands and wives, help each other train your mouth to speak only words of faith.

Instead of having a swear jar, have an unbelief and doubt jar. ... sounds cheesy, but try it. Every time something contrary to faith is spoken put money in the jar!

When your husband or wife corrects you and says, "That's a bad confession," don't become irritated. Just say, *"You're right. In the Name of Jesus, I rebuke that bad confession, and I render it powerless to come to pass!"* Help each other.

Speak whatever you desire to come to pass in the name of Jesus. Take authority over the money you need, and if you've been giving, command the harvest to come to you.

If you need healing, speak to your body. Command it to be healed in the name of Jesus. Command it to function properly. Speak the result you want. Whatever you say will come to pass.

You can't change your talk by simply going to church once a week. There is only one way you can achieve this and do so for the long term...by meditating on the Word of God, day and night. DAY AND NIGHT!

It's time to stop telling it like it is and start telling it like the Word of God says it should be. When you continually speak the Word of God in the face of adversity, you will change your circumstances.

Refuse to let the Devil or the world influence your words. Stand firm in your decision to only speak what you want to see come to pass in your life.

Don't forget Psalm 103:20, which tells us that angels move on His Word, heeding the "voice" of His Word. When you give voice to God's Word and speak His promises over your life...HEAVEN MOVES.

On the flip side, the enemy also moves to heed the "voice" of fear and unbelief. Think back to what Jesus said about it all in Matthew 12.

> "For by your words you will be justified and acquitted, and by your words you will be condemned and sentenced."
>
> — Matthew 12:37 (AMPC)

Chapter Eleven

Two Crazy Guys

This is possibly the greatest example of the producing power of words.

After exploring the land for forty days, the men returned to Moses, Aaron, and the whole community of Israel at Kadesh in the wilderness of Paran. They reported to the whole community what they had seen and showed them the fruit they had taken from the land. This was their report to Moses: "We entered the land you sent us to explore, and it is indeed a bountiful country—a land flowing with milk and honey. Here is the kind of fruit it produces. But the people living there are powerful, and their towns are large and fortified. We even saw giants there, the descendants of Anak! The Amalekites live in the Negev, and the Hittites, Jebusites, and Amorites live in the hill country. The Canaanites live along the coast of the Mediterranean Sea and along the Jordan Valley."

But Caleb tried to quiet the people as they stood before Moses.

"Let's go at once to take the land," he said. "We can certainly conquer it!"

But the other men who had explored the land with him disagreed. "We can't go up against them! They are stronger than we are!" So they spread this bad report about the land among the Israelites: "The land we traveled through and explored will devour anyone who goes to live there. All the people we saw were huge. We even saw giants there, the descendants of Anak. Next to them we felt like grasshoppers, and that's what they thought, too!"

— Numbers 13:25-33 (NLT)

Then the whole community began weeping aloud, and they cried all night. Their voices rose in a great chorus of protest against Moses and Aaron. "If only we had died in Egypt, or even here in the wilderness!" they complained. "Why is the Lord taking us to this country only to have us die in battle? Our wives and our little ones will be carried off as plunder! Wouldn't it be better for us to return to Egypt?" Then they plotted among themselves, "Let's choose a new leader and go back to Egypt!"

Then Moses and Aaron fell face down on the ground before the whole community of Israel. Two of the men who had explored the land, Joshua son of Nun and Caleb son of Jephunneh, tore their clothing. They said to all the people of Israel, "The land we traveled through and explored is a wonderful land! And if the Lord is pleased with us, he will bring us safely into that land and give it to us. It is a rich land flowing with milk and honey. Do not rebel against the Lord, and don't be afraid of the people of the land. They are only helpless prey to us! They have no protection, but the Lord is with us! Don't be afraid of them!"

But the whole community began to talk about stoning Joshua and Caleb. Then the glorious presence of the Lord appeared to all the Israelites at the Tabernacle. And the Lord said to Moses, "How long will these people treat me with contempt? Will they never believe me, even after all the miraculous signs I have done among them? I will disown them and destroy them with a plague. Then I will make you into a nation greater and mightier than they are!"

But Moses objected. "What will the Egyptians think when they hear about it?" he asked the Lord. "They know full well the power you displayed in rescuing your people from Egypt. Now if you destroy them, the Egyptians will send a report to the inhabitants of this land, who have already heard that you live among your people. They know, Lord, that you have appeared to your people face to face and that your pillar of cloud hovers over them. They know that you go before them in the pillar of cloud by day and the pillar of fire by night. Now if you slaughter all these people with a single blow, the nations that have heard of your fame will say, The Lord was not able to bring them into the land he swore to give them, so he killed them in the wilderness.'

"Please, Lord, prove that your power is as great as you have claimed. For you said, 'The Lord is slow to anger and filled with unfailing love, forgiving every kind of sin and rebellion. But he does not excuse the guilty. He lays the sins of the parents upon their children; the entire family is affected— even children in the third and fourth generations.' In keeping with your magnificent, unfailing love, please pardon the sins of this people, just as you have forgiven them ever since they left Egypt."

Then the Lord said, "I will pardon them as you have requested. But as surely as I live, and as surely as the earth is filled with the Lord's glory, not one of these people will ever enter that land. They have all seen my glorious presence and the miraculous signs I performed both in Egypt and in the wilderness, but again and again they have tested me by refusing to listen to my voice.

They will never even see the land I swore to give their ances-tors. None of those who have treated me with contempt will ever see it. But my servant Caleb has a different attitude than the others have. He has remained loyal to me, so I will bring him into the land he explored. His descendants will possess their full share of that land. Now turn around, and don't go on toward the land where the Amalekites and Canaanites live. Tomorrow you must set out for the wilder-ness in the direction of the Red Sea."

The Lord Punishes the Israelites

Then the Lord said to Moses and Aaron, "How long must I put up with this wicked community and its complaints about me? Yes, I have heard the complaints the Israelites are making against me. Now tell them this: 'As surely as I live, declares the Lord, I will do to you the very things I heard you say. You will all drop dead in this wilderness! Because you complained against me, every one of you who is twenty years old or older and was included in the registration will die. You will not enter and occupy the land I swore to give you. The only excep-tions will be Caleb son of Jephunneh and Joshua son of Nun.

"'You said your children would be carried off as plunder. Well, I will bring them safely into the land, and they will enjoy what you have despised. But as for you, you will drop dead in this wilderness. And your children will be like shepherds, wandering in the wilderness for forty years. In this way, they will pay for your faithlessness, until the last of you lies dead in the wilderness.

"'Because your men explored the land for forty days, you must

wander in the wilderness for forty years—a year for each day,
suffering the consequences of your sins. Then you will
discover what it is like to have me for an enemy. I, the Lord,
have spoken! I will certainly do these things to every
member of the community who has conspired against me.
They will be destroyed here in this wilderness, and here they
will die!"

The ten men Moses had sent to explore the land—the ones who
incited rebellion against the Lord with their bad report—
were struck dead with a plague before the Lord. Of the
twelve who had explored the land, only Joshua and Caleb
remained alive.

— Numbers 14:1-38 (NLT)

God said that He would do the very thing THEY CONFESSED.

Caleb had just returned from spying out the Promised Land. And all
the spies who had gone there with him, except for Joshua, had
returned with "an evil report." They acknowledged that the land was
good and flowing with milk and honey, but they SAID it would be
impossible to conquer. When the Israelites heard that news, they
started weeping and wailing.

But Caleb interrupted them. *"Wait a minute! If the Lord is pleased with us,
he will lead us into that land...and will give it to us"* (Numbers 14:8). Caleb
wasn't just being positive—God had already promised to give them the
land. He was declaring God's Word and saying by faith, "We can do
this!"

Those with a bad report were speaking in unbelief. They not only said,
"We cannot do this!" They said, "We might as well have died in the
wilderness!" You can read how it ended...the entire generation of

doubters died in the wilderness, but Caleb claimed the land and walked right into it. Everyone there GOT WHAT THEY SAID.

Saying and believing is God's plan of dominion. It's how we, as Christians, got born again. And now that we're saved, we're supposed to receive all His other BLESSINGS by using the same process. *{If you are not born again, the bonus chapter is just for you}*

Sadly, many believers haven't been doing that. They've just gone along passively and unhappily with whatever happens to them, not using the power of their words to change it.

Someone might say: "I've never been a fan of making faith confessions. I like to leave everything up to God. He's really the One who chooses what happens in our lives."

No, He's not. He's given that choice to us.

> But the word is very near you, in your mouth and in your
>   mind and in your heart, so that you can do it.
> See, I have set before you this day life and good, and death and
>   evil.
> I call heaven and earth to witness this day against you that I
>   have set before you life and death, the blessings and the
>   curses; therefore choose life, that you and your descendants
>   may live.
>
> — Deuteronomy 30:14-15, 19 (AMPC)

Just like the Israelites, we can give a bad report or a good report. And in the end, we will have what we say. So, let's exchange wrong words for the right ones and a bad report for a good and faith-filled report.

I guess you can say "ABRACADABRA." Yup. I said it. I said "Abra-cadabra." And you're probably wondering what in the world I'm trying to prove here.

When I say "ABRACADABRA" what comes to your mind? How do you initially define it?...Magic?...Witchcraft? ...Harry Potter? ...Disney?

Did you know this is a Hebrew word? And do you know what's even crazier? It means "I create as I speak."

Sound familiar? ...sounds like what God did in Genesis 1. It's actually taken from Numbers 12:13, where Moses started declaring "I pray healing, I pray healing" over Miriam.

This isn't some chant nonsense. Moses understood the creative power of his words. He understood that he creates as he speaks.

I could go further with this. But if you dig more into this Hebrew word, you'll even see that "BARA" which is used in Genesis to describe the word "CREATE" is encapsulated in abracadabra. Also, the name of God is wrapped in it.

It's just like the Devil to hitch to something that is originally meant to be holy. You create as you speak!

Chapter Twelve

God Slapped His Mouth Shut

Read the following passage slowly and see what God is showing you. It's crucial. What we see God do to Zechariah here is huge.

> When Herod was king of Judea, there was a Jewish priest named Zechariah. He was a member of the priestly order of Abijah, and his wife, Elizabeth, was also from the priestly line of Aaron. Zechariah and Elizabeth were righteous in God's eyes, careful to obey all of the Lord's commandments and regulations. They had no children because Elizabeth was unable to conceive, and they were both very old.
> One day Zechariah was serving God in the Temple, for his order was on duty that week. As was the custom of the priests, he was chosen by lot to enter the sanctuary of the Lord and burn incense. While the incense was being burned, a great crowd stood outside, praying.
> While Zechariah was in the sanctuary, an angel of the Lord appeared to him, standing to the right of the incense altar. Zechariah was shaken and overwhelmed with fear

when he saw him. But the angel said, "Don't be afraid,
Zechariah! God has heard your prayer. Your wife, Elizabeth,
will give you a son, and you are to name him John. You will
have great joy and gladness, and many will rejoice at his
birth, for he will be great in the eyes of the Lord. He must
never touch wine or other alcoholic drinks. He will be filled
with the Holy Spirit, even before his birth. And he will turn
many Israelites to the Lord their God.

He will be a man with the spirit and power of Elijah. He will
prepare the people for the coming of the Lord. He will turn
the hearts of the fathers to their children, and he will cause
those who are rebellious to accept the wisdom of the godly."

Zechariah said to the angel, "How can I be sure this will
happen? I'm an old man now, and my wife is also well along
in years."

Then the angel said, "I am Gabriel! I stand in the very presence
of God. It was he who sent me to bring you this good
news! But now, since you didn't believe what I said, you will
be silent and unable to speak until the child is born. For my
words will certainly be fulfilled at the proper time."

Meanwhile, the people were waiting for Zechariah to come out
of the sanctuary, wondering why he was taking so
long. When he finally did come out, he couldn't speak to
them. Then they realized from his gestures and his silence
that he must have seen a vision in the sanctuary.

When Zechariah's week of service in the Temple was over, he
returned home. Soon afterward his wife, Elizabeth, became
pregnant and went into seclusion for five months. "How
kind the Lord is!" she exclaimed. "He has taken away my
disgrace of having no children."

— Luke 1:5-25 (NLT)

Notice that Zechariah slipped into unbelief and doubt. And as a result, God slapped his mouth shut. WHY? The angel explains why in verse 20: *"for my words will certainly be fulfilled."*

The angel was saying, "I have to close your mouth, because if you speak, your words will produce something contrary to mine, and John must be born!"

The angel gave a crash course on the producing power of words. Words are so powerful that they can abort what God wants to birth in your life. Make sure your mouth is speaking forth God's best.

Afterword

The words you say will either acquit you or condemn you. — Matthew 12:37 (NLT)

The tongue can bring life or death. — Proverbs 18:21 (NLT)

Your words contain meaning and power in your life. They have creative power, just as God showed when He created the Heavens and the Earth with His words. Now, you have the authority to do the same thing here on Earth.

Take control of your life by getting control of your tongue. Refuse to speak anything other than the Word of God about your life or situation.

Now, page ahead to check out the daily declarations.

Daily Declarations

You shall also decide and decree a thing, and it shall be established for you; and the light [of God's favor] shall shine upon your ways.

—Job 22:28 (AMPC)

I DECLARE my position is changing to my next level. I established every desire of my heart today. I will never suffer shame and reproach anymore. I will find myself where I least expect. I will encounter favor this week. It will be forward ever, backward never for me and my home, in Jesus' name.

I DECLARE the root of sickness and disease is destroyed in my life and home today. The yoke of physical and mental sickness will be destroyed today. Every form of pain and discomfort will not be in my home, in Jesus' name.

I DECLARE whatever has kept me in frustration and stagnation, God will rise on my behalf and execute vengeance. Every agent of the Devil bugging my destiny ends now in Jesus' name. Every gang of evil gathered against my family, children, career, and health, today I decree them crushed in the mighty name of Jesus. Every planting of evil tormenting my life, I decree instant judgment and my speedy recovery in the name of Jesus.

I DECLARE no force of Hell will resist my advancement anymore in the name of Jesus. From today, every issue of pity surrounding my life is turned into a testimony of victory. This is my week of testimonies, in Jesus' name.

I DECLARE someone needs my difference. I am necessary. God made me an original, so I will not be a copy. I am authentic. I am fearfully and wonderfully made. I carry something so extraordinary. My divine assignment and my purpose is powerful. I am a divine ingredient placed on the Earth, in Jesus' name.

I DECLARE God's incredible blessings over my life. I will see an explosion of God's goodness, a sudden widespread increase. I will experience the unsurpassed greatness of God's favor. It will elevate me to a level higher than I ever dreamed of. Explosive blessings are coming my way, in Jesus' name.

I DECLARE I will experience God's faithfulness. I will not worry. I will not doubt. I will keep my trust in Him, knowing that He will not fail me. I will give birth to every promise God put in my heart, and I will become everything God created me to be, in Jesus' name.

I DECLARE I have the grace I need for today. I am full of power, strength, and determination. Nothing I face will be too much for me. I will overcome every obstacle, outlast every challenge, and come through every difficulty better off than I was before, in Jesus' name.

I DECLARE that it is not too late to accomplish everything God has placed in my heart. I have not missed my window of opportunity. God has moments of favor in my future. He is preparing me right now because He is about to release a special grace to help me accomplish that dream. This is my time. This is my moment, in Jesus' name.

I DECLARE that I am grateful for who God is in my life and for what He's done. I will not take for granted the people, the opportunities, and the favor He has blessed me with. I will look at what is right and not what is wrong. I will thank Him for what I have and not complain about what I don't have. I will see each day as a gift from God. My heart will overflow with praise and gratitude for all of His goodness, in Jesus' name.

I DECLARE a legacy of faith over my life. I declare I will store up blessings for future generations. My life is marked by excellence and integrity. Because I'm making right choices and taking steps of faith, others will want to follow me. God's abundance is surrounding my life today, in Jesus' name.

I DECLARE that God has a great plan for my life. He is directing my steps. Even though I may not always understand how, I know my situation is not a surprise to God. He will work out every detail to my advantage. In His perfect timing, everything will turn out right, in Jesus' name.

I DECLARE that God's dream for my life is coming to pass. It will not be stopped by people, disappointments, or adversities. God has solutions to every problem I will ever face. The right people and the right breaks are in my future. I will fulfill my destiny, in Jesus' name.

I DECLARE that I refuse to be afraid for my children/grandchildren. I surround them with faith and with the love of God. I see them as successful, happy, protected, and healthy. Whenever I think of my children and their future, I have a sound mind. I picture them surrounded by God's power and love, in Jesus' name.

I DECLARE that our family walks in love. My relationship with my children/grandchildren is blessed. We walk in love with each other and enjoy each other as God intended. We don't allow strife or division, but declare that our home is filled with peace and harmony, in Jesus' name.

I DECLARE that my children/grandchildren are hungry for God. I declare that my children/grandchildren love God and are sensitive to His voice. They are hungry for the things of the Spirit. Revelation from God flows to them. They see and understand spiritual things. They know what God has called them to do, and they want to do it, in Jesus' name.

I DECLARE my children/grandchildren are overcomers. God's plan for them is greater than any plan or force of the enemy. God causes my children/grandchildren to overcome every life situation, in Jesus' name.

I DECLARE that peace reigns in the hearts and minds of my children/grandchildren. My children/grandchildren are whole, and complete, with nothing lacking, and nothing lost. The peace of God guides them and keeps them. My children have great peace in their lives, in Jesus' name.

I DECLARE that my children/grandchildren are diligent. My children/grandchildren are not lazy but good workers who persevere. They are steady, earnest, and energetic. Because of that, they will not be poor but rich, according to God's Word, in Jesus' name.

I DECLARE that my mind and thoughts are covered by the blood of Jesus. By that same blood, I overcome the Devil. I am made perfect through the blood of the everlasting covenant. I have boldness to enter into the presence of God through that blood, in Jesus' name.

I DECLARE that I receive my benefits of the new covenant through the blood of Jesus. I receive healing and health through the blood of Jesus. I receive abundance and prosperity through the blood of Jesus. I receive deliverance through the blood of Jesus, and I break the power of sin and iniquity in my life through the blood of Jesus, in Jesus' name.

I DECLARE that my marriage is blessed. My home is blessed. My spouse is blessed and highly favored. Everything they do prospers. God is with them. They are sensitive to the leading and directing of the Holy Spirit, in Jesus' name.

I DECLARE that my body is the Temple of the Holy Spirit. I have been bought with a price. Therefore, I will glorify God with how I treat my body. The life of God flows through me. I am healthy, and I am disciplined with my body, in Jesus' name.

I DECLARE the Lord is my Refuge and my Fortress. He delivers my enemies. Therefore, I do not fear the terror in the night nor the destruction that takes place at noonday. Angels are given charge over me. I am blessed in my coming and going. The Holy Spirit comforts me, in Jesus' name.

I DECLARE that I walk in the favor of God. And my favor is increasing even as I speak. I am the head and not the tail, above and never beneath in every case. I'm ever moving forward. My life will never go backward, in Jesus' name.

I DECLARE I am established in God's Word. I am preserved from trouble. I overcome trouble through the Blood of Jesus and the word of my testimony. No weapon formed against me will win. Every tongue that rises up against me will be condemned, in Jesus' name.

I DECLARE I operate with integrity. I actively seek and live in God's wisdom. I will not allow corrupt communication to proceed out of my mouth. Wealth and riches are in my house. I am empowered to win because of the anointing upon my life. I am anointed. I am increasing in the anointing today. I associate with those who value and honor the anointing, in Jesus' name.

I DECLARE that there will be no mourning or death in my home. The Lord will make a difference between my home and the world. All through this month and all through this year, nothing will fail in my hands. All year I will never know setback, in Jesus' name.

I DECLARE that this year will be my year of joy and laughter. No battle will stand before me. My life will keep burning brighter through this year. And anything broken in my life and family is restored now, in Jesus' Name.

I DECLARE that I have the grace to make the Kingdom of God my priority. And as I favor the Kingdom, I will experience a greater level of Kingdom favor. I will win on every side. The attack on my business and career is over now. Nothing fails in my life. This year will be stress-free, in Jesus' Name.

These are scriptures that I compiled. You can do the same. Find scriptures that cover your case or situation and write them down. THEN DECLARE THEM!

Do You Know Jesus?

Jesus loves you!

If you're depressed, he can give you joy to the full. If you're troubled, he can give you peace.

You may have started out going the wrong way, but you don't have to keep going that way. You can choose Christ now and get on the right track.

There's not one issue God can't answer for you. You are only one decision away from God turning your life around for the better. No one has ever come to Jesus, and their life got worse; their life always got better.

What do you need to do?

1. Repent toward Jesus and away from sin.

2. Confess Jesus as Lord and Savior

3. Receive Jesus by faith and live committed to His teaching.

Why not give your life to Christ now? The Bible tells us that God is not willing that any should perish, but that all should come to repentance.

Pray this prayer:

Dear Heavenly Father,
Thank you for your Son, Jesus Christ. Jesus…thank you for coming and dying on the cross for me. I confess you TODAY as Lord and Savior of my life. Come into my heart and cleanse me of all my sin. Connect me to my new beginning. I believe you are alive, that God raised you up. I declare that you are the King of Kings and Lord of Lords. In Jesus' name, I have prayed. AMEN!

Congratulations on the best decision of your life! I have had regrets, but choosing Jesus was never one of them. Welcome to your best life.

If you prayed this prayer, please let me know. Email me: HLCC@LIVE.CA

- Get into a good church.
- Find yourself a Bible and read it daily.
- Talk to God every day.
- Tell others about the hope you found in Christ.

About the Author

Philip Hutchings' passion and love for God and God's Word connect to his desire to be used in bringing in the final harvest of souls on the Earth today and see the worldwide church in revival. After graduating from Zion Bible College in Barrington, R.I. in 2004, Philip has encouraged and helped many men, women, and children of many nationalities. The unique delivery of the spoken Word through Philip has released the power of God to see transformation in many lives. Philip and his wife Jamie felt impressed of the Lord to birth a church in Saint John, New Brunswick, Canada called Higher Life Church, and he continues to pastor and minister with his team. After going to jail and being put into solitary confinement for seven days for refusing to close the church during COVID, God has given him a national platform to preach the Gospel and see hope restored in the Church across Canada.

 facebook.com/higherlifecanada

twitter.com/HLChurchCanada

Printed in the USA
CPSIA information can be obtained
at www.ICGtesting.com
LVHW041543280723
753393LV00004B/955